INSIDE YOUR BODY

ALL ABOUT EAR INFECTIONS

FRANCESCA POTTS, RN

Consulting Editor, Diane Craig, MA/Reading Specialist

Super Sandcastle

An Imprint of Abdo Publishing
abdopublishing.com

ABDOPUBLISHING.COM

Published by Abdo Publishing, a division of ABDO, PO Box 398166, Minneapolis, Minnesota 55439. Copyright © 2018 by Abdo Consulting Group, Inc. International copyrights reserved in all countries. No part of this book may be reproduced in any form without written permission from the publisher. Super SandCastle™ is a trademark and logo of Abdo Publishing.

Printed in the United States of America,
North Mankato, Minnesota
062017
092017

Production: Mighty Media, Inc.
Editor: Megan Borgert-Spaniol
Cover Photographs: iStock, Shutterstock
Interior Photographs: iStock; Mighty Media, Inc.; Shutterstock

Publisher's Cataloging-in-Publication Data
Names: Potts, Francesca, author.
Title: All about ear infections / by Francesca Potts, RN.
Description: Minneapolis, MN : Abdo Publishing, 2018. I Series:
   Inside your body
Identifiers: LCCN 2016962912 I ISBN 9781532111198 (lib. bdg.) I
   ISBN 9781680789041 (ebook)
Subjects: LCSH: Otitis media in children--Juvenile literature. I
   Pediatric otology--Juvenile literature. I Pediatric otolaryngology--
   Juvenile literature.
Classification: DDC 618.92--dc23
LC record available at http://lccn.loc.gov/2016962912

Super SandCastle™ books are created by a team of professional educators, reading specialists, and content developers around five essential components—phonemic awareness, phonics, vocabulary, text comprehension, and fluency—to assist young readers as they develop reading skills and strategies and increase their general knowledge. All books are written, reviewed, and leveled for guided reading, early reading intervention, and Accelerated Reader™ programs for use in shared, guided, and independent reading and writing activities to support a balanced approach to literacy instruction.

CONTENTS

YOUR BODY

YOUR EARS

You're amazing! So is your body.
Most of the time your body works just fine.
It lets you go to school, play with friends,
and more. But sometimes you feel sick or
part of you hurts.

our ears are made up of many different parts. They all work together to help you hear. But sometimes your ears are hurt or **infected**. Ear infections are common in kids like you.

ALL ABOUT
EAR
INFECTIONS

Ear **infections** are unhealthy conditions inside the ear. They can occur in the outer, middle, or inner ear.

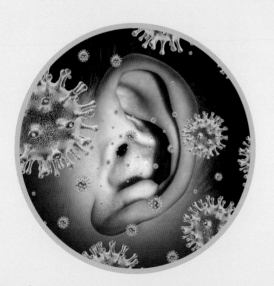

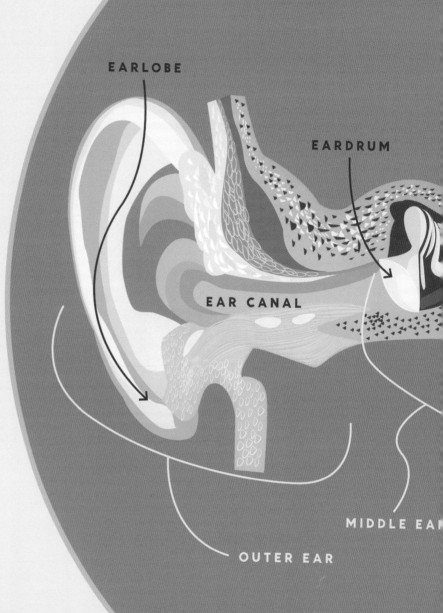

EARLOBE

EARDRUM

EAR CANAL

MIDDLE EAR

OUTER EAR

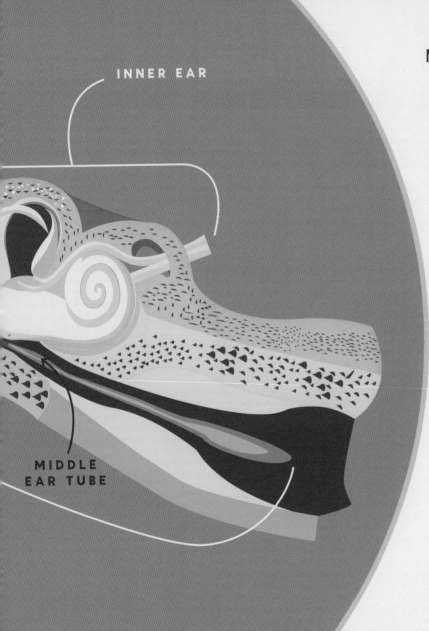

INNER EAR

MIDDLE
EAR TUBE

Most **infections** are in the middle ear. The tube in your middle ear lets air move in and out. But sometimes **fluid** gets trapped inside the tube. This makes it easier for **germs** to grow there.

"Oto" Means Ear

Words beginning with "oto-" are related to ears. An otoscope is a tool used to look at the inside of the ear.

HEALTHY EARS

Healthy ears do a lot to keep you comfortable. Earwax and ear popping are two signs that your ears are doing their job!

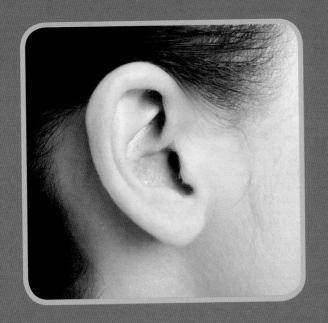

Earwax

Earwax is produced in the outer ear. Do not stick a cotton swab in your ear to clean it out! Earwax helps keep your ears moist and clean.

Ear Popping

Have you ever flown in an airplane? You probably felt a pop in your ears. This popping is your ears adapting to changes in **air pressure**.

CAUSES

Ear **infections** are caused by a virus or bacteria in the ear. They often occur when the body is already sick. A cold or flu can cause the middle ear tube to swell. Then **fluid** builds up. This makes it easy for bacteria or viruses to spread.

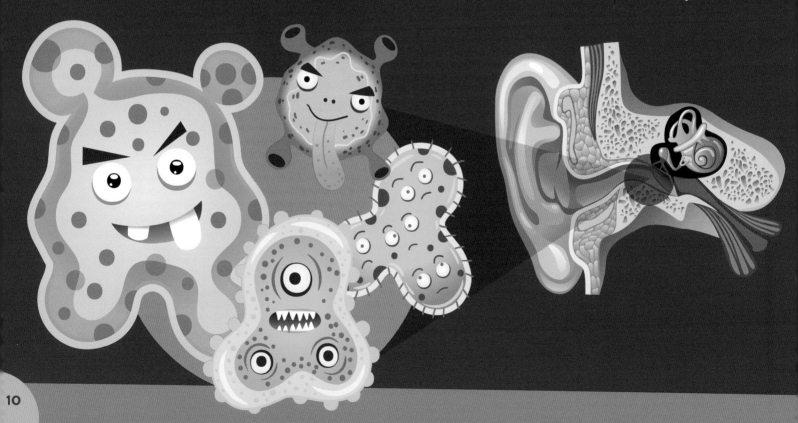

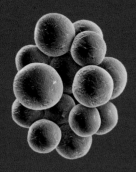

Bacteria

Bacteria are **germs** that spread in or outside of the body. They can cause illnesses. Strep throat is caused by bacteria.

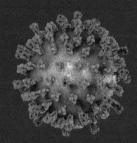

Viruses

Viruses are germs that need to be inside living things to survive. Humans are often their hosts! Viruses also cause illnesses. The flu and common cold are caused by viruses.

FAST FACT

Kids get ear **infections** more often than adults. One reason for this is their ear tubes are shorter and flatter. It is easier for germs to get stuck inside!

SIGNS
AND SYMPTOMS

The **symptoms** of an ear **infection** can vary. They may depend on which part of the ear is affected.

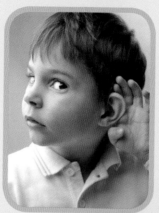

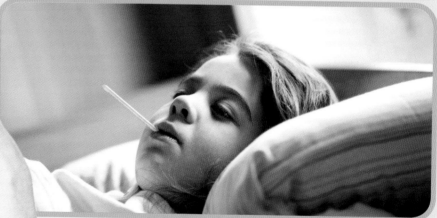

MOST COMMON EAR INFECTION SYMPTOMS

EAR PAIN

FEELING LIKE THERE IS WATER STUCK IN YOUR EAR

RED, SWOLLEN EAR

FEVER

TROUBLE HEARING

FLUID DRAINING FROM EAR

HEADACHE

DIZZINESS OR LOSS OF BALANCE

CHRONIC
EAR INFECTIONS

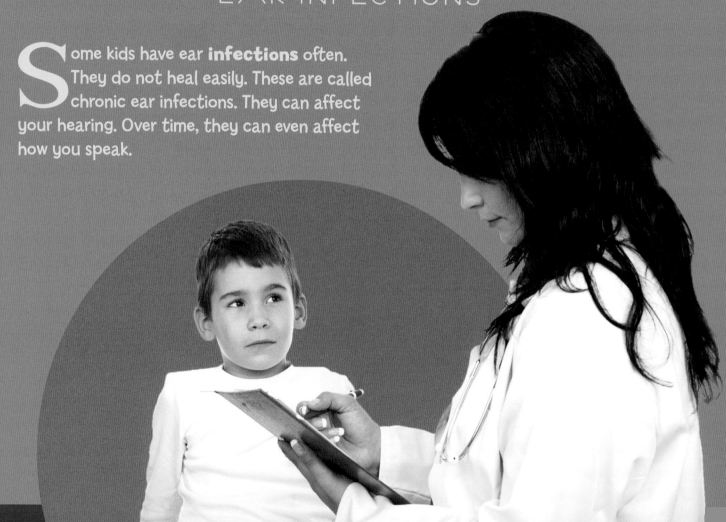

Some kids have ear **infections** often. They do not heal easily. These are called chronic ear infections. They can affect your hearing. Over time, they can even affect how you speak.

Ear tube **surgery** is a common way to treat chronic ear **infections**. During the surgery, the doctor places a plastic or metal tube into your **eardrum**. The tube helps **fluid** flow out of the ear. This prevents fluid from building up. It also improves your hearing!

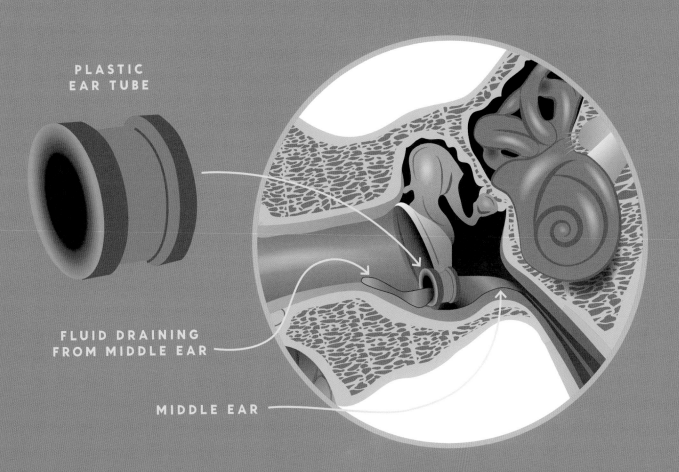

PLASTIC
EAR TUBE

FLUID DRAINING
FROM MIDDLE EAR

MIDDLE EAR

TREATMENT

HOW DO YOU TREAT AN EAR INFECTION?

REST

MEDICINE TO TREAT SYMPTOMS

ANTIBIOTICS FOR BACTERIAL INFECTIONS

EAR TUBE SURGERY FOR CHRONIC EAR INFECTIONS

Bacterial or Viral?

Antibiotics will not work if your ear **infection** is caused by a virus. Only time and rest can make you better. The good news? Ear infections often last just a day or two. You will feel better in no time!

Do you think you have an ear infection?

You should go to your doctor if:

- You have bad ear pain

- **Fluid**, **pus**, or blood **drains** from your ear

- **Symptoms** do not go away after **treatment**

MEDICINES

AND REMEDIES

Your doctor may give you **antibiotics**. You can also find ear drops and pain relievers at the store. These medicines help you stay comfortable while your body fights the **infection**.

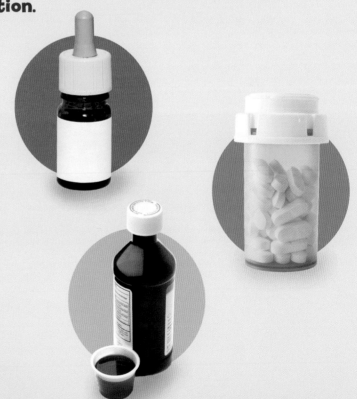

There are also ways to ease your **symptoms** at home.

- Press a heating pad or warm cloth to your ear.

- Rub your face, jaw, and neck with lavender oil or other plant oils.

- **Gargle** with salt water.

- Keep your head up! This helps **fluid** flow out of your ears.

RUPTURED
EARDRUM

An ear **infection** can cause **pus** to build up in your middle ear. Too much pus can make your **eardrum** rupture, or tear. If your eardrum ruptures, you will know! It usually comes with sharp pain and brief loss of hearing.

Surgery is sometimes needed to fix a torn **eardrum**. But the eardrum usually heals on its own.

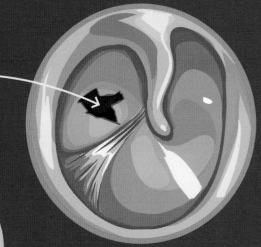

RUPTURED
EARDRUM

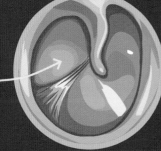

NORMAL
EARDRUM

Be Careful!

Poking inside your ear with a cotton swab can tear your eardrum. So can loud noises and sudden changes in **air pressure**.

PREVENTION

Ear **infections** cannot be passed from person to person. But the illnesses that cause them often can! You can help prevent ear infections by trying to stay healthy.

KEEP YOUR EARS DRY AND CLEAN.

WASH YOUR HANDS.

AVOID CIGARETTE SMOKE.

AVOID FRIENDS AND FAMILY MEMBERS WHO ARE SICK.

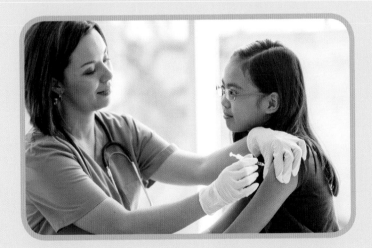

GET A FLU SHOT EVERY YEAR.

We all get sick from time to time. But remember that your body is amazing. It is always working to help you feel better!

GLOSSARY

AIR PRESSURE – the weight of air as it pushes on objects.

ANTIBIOTIC – a substance used to kill germs that cause disease.

DRAIN – to flow out.

EARDRUM – a thin membrane between the middle and outer ear.

FLUID – a liquid.

GARGLE – to hold a liquid in the throat and make it bubble with air from the lungs.

GERM – a tiny, living organism that can make people sick.

INFECTED – having an infection. An infection is an unhealthy condition caused by bacteria or other germs.

PUS – a thick, yellowish substance the body produces when it becomes infected.

SURGERY – the treating of sickness or injury by cutting into and repairing body parts.

SYMPTOM – a noticeable change in the normal working of the body.

TREATMENT – medical or surgical care for a sickness or an injury.